A Special Day for Mommies

The Origin of Mother's Day

Holiday Book for Kids
Children's Holiday Books

BABY PROFESSOR

EDUCATION KIDS

In this book we'll learn more about Mother's Day. For many of us, that's a day when we bring Mom breakfast in bed, or a bouquet of flowers. But when did this practice start? What's it all about?

HAPPY
Mother's Day

HONORING MOTHERS

Mother's Day in the United States became an official holiday in 1914, and usually falls on the second Sunday in May. But many cultures, over many centuries, have had special times to honor mothers. The ancient Greeks and Romans held annual festivals to honor their mother goddesses, Rhea and Cybele, and families gave special honor to the mothers in their households at that time.

For Christians in Europe and especially England, the fourth Sunday in Lent, usually in March or April, became a day to honor Mary, the mother of Jesus Christ. Then "Mothering Sunday" evolved into a ceremony to honor the

"mother church", and people would travel to the church in the town where they had grown up for a service on that day.

In the early twentieth century, the meaning of Mothering Sunday changed again, and it became more of a day for taking flowers to your own mother and perhaps having a special meal with her. By the middle of the twentieth century, Mothering Sunday in Europe had become almost the same as Mother's Day in North America.

MOTHER'S DAY MOVEMENTS

In the United States, Ann Jarvis started work groups in the 1860s to help women learn how to be better mothers. After the Civil War, these groups played a major part in Virginia and nearby states to help restore communities where some had supported the Union and others the Confederate forces. In 1868 Jarvis sponsored Mothers' Friendship Day, bringing together mothers with their children who had fought on both sides in the war.

In 1870, Julia Ward Howe called for American women to unite for world peace, and to oppose any future adventures that would send their children off to war again. She wanted June 2 to be an annual holiday, Mother's Peace Day.

In Michigan, Juliet Calhoun Blakely started an annual mother's day event in Albion in the 1870s. The event was closely tied with the temperance movement, which fought against the wide use of alcohol in society.

In 1905, Anna Jarvis wanted some way to honor her mother, Ann, who had recently died. She thought a national holiday would help all families remember the mothers, both living and dead, and their part in family and national life.

Re
those
kids a
You made

Jarvis gained support both locally and with several important sponsors. The first official Mother's Day of her movement took place at a church in West Virginia and, at the same time, at an event in a department store in Philadelphia. The event at the store drew thousands of people, far more than the organizers had expected. This helped to prove the popularity of the idea.

Jarvis argued that almost every United States holiday, besides religious holidays and the Fourth of July, celebrated men. She created a movement to establish Mother's Day as an official holiday. By 1912 many churches and towns, and even some states, were celebrating Mother's Day. The holiday finally got on the official calendar in 1914, when President Wilson signed a bill into law establishing Mother's Day as the second Sunday in May.

Happy
Mother's
Day

MOTHER'S DAY TRADITIONS

*A*nna Jarvis wanted Mother's Day to be a time for people to be with or remember their mothers, and honor their sacrifice and hard work. However, once Mother's Day became an official holiday, many people began to see ways to make money off it.

Florists advertise sending flowers, and greeting-card manufacturers urge you to buy and send a card instead of making one yourself. Restaurants offer special meals your could take mom to enjoy.

MOM

HAPPY
MOTHE
DA

Anna Jarvis opposed making money off the holiday, and even sued companies that used "Mother's Day" in their advertising. By the 1940s she thought Mother's Day had changed into something she did not recognize, and tried to have it removed as an official holiday. But by that time, the event was very popular and had taken on a life of its own.

In the United States, children often make breakfast for their moms, or make or buy little gifts for them. Only Christmas is a bigger gift-giving day. In many houses, it's a day when dad and the kids do all the chores like washing the dishes and making the beds, so mom does not have to. If the weather is nice, it's a great day to take mom for a picnic—as long as she does not have to do all the preparing and cleaning up after.

Mother's Day, according to telephone companies, is the day in the year with the greatest number of phone calls. People living far away from home call mom to say hi, and perhaps to share some memories of when they were small and how their mom cared for them.

Sometimes people use Mother's Day as a time to talk about an issue important to women. In 1968, Coretta Scott King headed a Mother's Day march to draw attention to the needs of poor mothers and their children. In the 1970s several Mother's Day events called for access to better child care, and for equal rights for women.

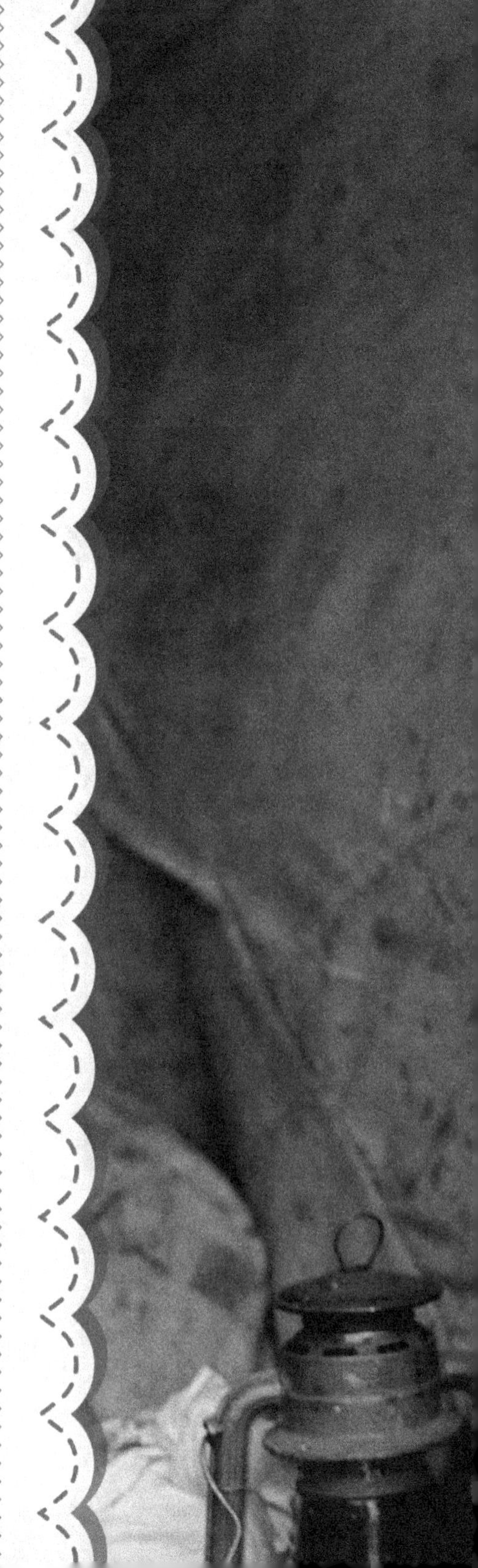

MOTHER'S DAY AROUND THE WORLD

There is no one right way to honor our mothers and the work they do, and no one time of the year. In different countries, events of different kinds take place.

In Argentina, Mother's Day is in October, and used to be related to a religious celebration of the Mother of Jesus. That celebration has moved to a different time in the year, but Mother's Day stayed in October as a popular tradition.

In Ethiopia, the mothers' celebration is a three-day event called **Antrosht**, at the end of the rainy season (usually in October). There are special foods and songs, and the mothers rub butter on their faces to make them shiny.

Happy
Mother's
Day

In France and Germany at the start of the twentieth century, the governments saw celebrating Mother's Day as a way to encourage mothers to have more babies. They gave out medals and money to women with lots of babies, and honored them with parades and concerts. Now, Mother's Day in those countries is much as it is in the U.S.

Indonesian Mother's Day is in December, and started in 1953 as a way to celebrate the spirit of the nation in general and the part women play in particular. Now it is more a family celebration, and involves surprise parties, special gifts and meals, and letting mom spend a day without having to work.

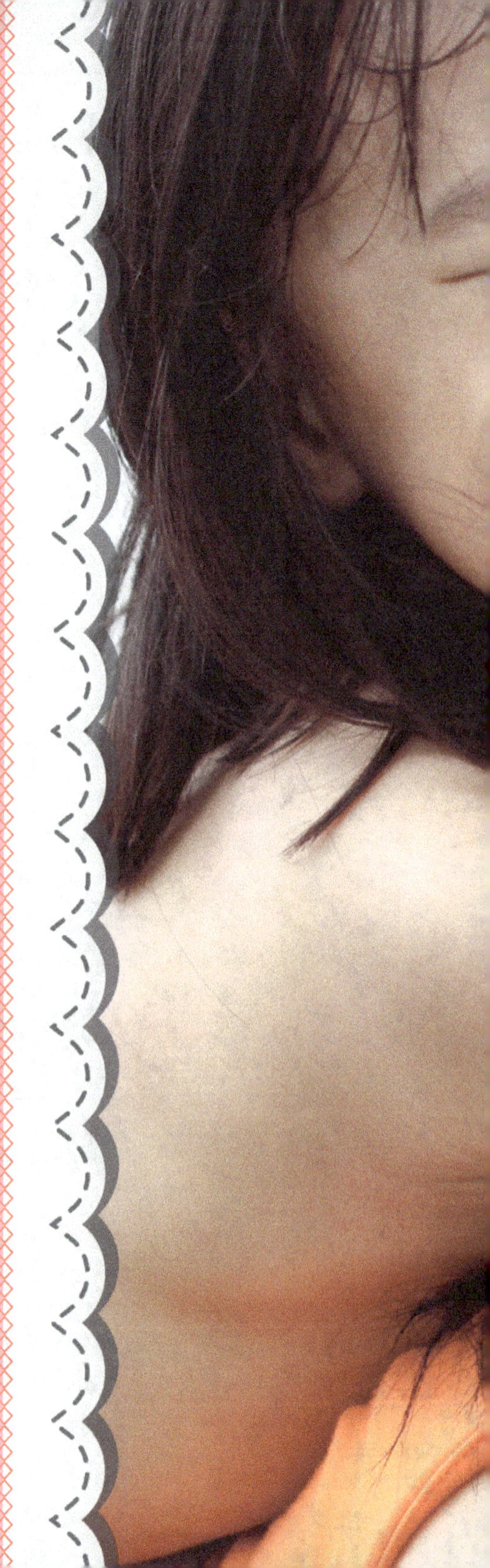

Queen Sirikit

In Thailand, Mother's Day is on the birthday of Queen Sirikit, the queen mother. She has been queen since 1956, and many people in Thailand think of her as the mother of the country.

Japan's Mother's Day used to be in March, and was connected with the birthday of the Emperor's wife. Now the holiday is in May, and the tradition is to give or send flowers like roses to your mother.

Happy
Mother's
Day!

Mother's Day only started in Malta after 1961, but now it is one of the most popular holidays in the country. Families usually take mom to a special restaurant to enjoy a fancy meal.

For "Dia de las Madres" each May in Mexico, families start the day with the song "Las Mañanitas". Families either join together for a big restaurant meal, or organize a meal at home with every family member bringing a contribution.

Television and radio networks in Pakistan run special programs in honor of Mother's Day, featuring stories of famous and little-known women who worked faithfully for their families and their nation.

In Russia, the big celebration is International Women's Day. It focuses more on the role women play to build up society, rather than their role as wives and mothers.

Swedish Mother's Day is at the end of May. This gives everyone a better chance to go outside in warmer weather to find flowers to make into a gift for mom, rather than having to buy them.

In Nepal, there is a festival called The Mothers' New Moon Pilgrimage. It happens over several days each April or May, and involves gift-giving to mothers and remembering mothers who have died.

Mother's Day in Egypt and other Arab countries is on March 21, the first day of spring. People sing popular songs in honor of mothers and motherhood.

In China, the government uses Mother's Day to remind people in cities of the needs of poor women in the country and in the west of China. People send carnations and lilies to their mothers. The lilies remind people of an ancient custom: when children left home, their mothers would plant lilies near the house in their honor.

LEARN MORE ABOUT CELEBRATIONS

What does your family do for Mother's Day? How about your friends? In other Baby Professor books you can learn about other holidays and customs from all around the world.

Visit
BABY PROFESSOR
EDUCATION KIDS
www.BabyProfessorBooks.com
to download Free Baby Professor eBooks and view
our catalog of new and exciting Children's Books

www.ingramcontent.com/pod-product-compliance
Lightning Source LLC
Chambersburg PA
CBHW060127120726
48003CB00009B/2797